P
IN THE PULPIT

Henry C. Fish

THE BANNER OF TRUTH TRUST

THE BANNER OF TRUTH TRUST

3 Murrayfield Road, Edinburgh EH12 6EL, UK
PO Box 621, Carlisle, PA 17013, USA

*

© The Banner of Truth Trust 2013

*

ISBN:
Print: 978-1-84871-307-9
EPUB: 978-1-84871-305-5
Kindle: 978-1-84871-306-2

*

Typeset in 10/13 pt Sabon Oldstyle Figures
at The Banner of Truth Trust, Edinburgh.

Printed in the USA by
Versa Press, Inc.,
East Peoria, IL.

POWER IN THE PULPIT

When God called Aaron to the office of high priest, he said, as a reason, 'I know that he can speak well.' The reason was weighty. Speech is a mighty power. It is God's chief instrument in salvation. God's word at first created the world, and his word, from the lips of his servants, is to re-create it. Ministers are speakers by profession. With them, therefore, power of speech is of the highest moment. It was never so needful as now. The churches want[1] many things, but nothing so much as increased power in their pulpits. It is an era of progress; and if other agencies have increased power, the pulpit must have it or lose its supremacy. It is an active, busy, noisy age; and if the pulpit would be heard, it must lift up its voice like a trumpet. It is a pretentious age; and if errorists will obtrude their false views and theories, then must the pulpit meet and explode them. It is a wicked age; and if the current of vice is to be arrested, then must the pulpit be foremost, with the soul-penetrating dispensations of the Word.

But let us do honour to the Holy Spirit. The preacher, while, like other speakers, he has power to inform and excite an audience, has not power in himself to compass the great aim of preaching. The aim of preaching is different from that of other public speaking. It looks deeper. It would renew and cleanse the heart. If it fails here, it fails entirely. And fail it will without the

[1] Lack.

accompanying 'power from on high'. The renewal of the soul is what no man, with all the wealth of learning and scholarship, and of cultivated taste and oratorical power, can accomplish. It is 'not by might, nor by power, but by my Spirit', saith the Lord. A sermon may be constructed after the best models; it may conform to all the rules of homiletics; the text may be suitable and fruitful; the plan may be faultless; the execution may discover genius and judgment; there may be accurate analysis and strong reasoning; proof and motive; solidity and beauty; logic and passion; argument direct and indirect; perspicuity, purity, correctness, propriety, precision; description, antithesis, metaphor, allegory, comparison; motives from goodness, motives from happiness, motives from self-love; appeals to the sense of the beautiful, the sense of right, to the affections, the passions, the emotions; a sermon may be all this, and yet that very sermon, even though it fell from the lips of a prince of pulpit oratory, were as powerless in the renewal of a soul as in raising of the dead, if unaccompanied by the omnipotent energy of the Holy Ghost.

But while the power which gives preaching success is supernatural, there are efficient modes of preaching the gospel, and inefficient modes. There are laws of persuasion; rules for influencing the mind. And these are appointed of God. Is it too much to suppose, then, that the influences of the Holy Spirit are more likely to be given in respecting these laws, than in the violation of them? Of Paul and Barnabas, it is said, in a particular instance, 'They *so spake* that a great multitude, both of the Jews and also of the Gentiles, believed.' Though a sovereign, yet the divine Being is not an arbitrary sovereign; and it cannot be denied that there is a general connection between the means and the end in the operations of grace, as well as in those of nature. What, therefore, would affect a man *without* the Spirit, we might expect to be employed *by* the Spirit to carry conviction to the heart. Otherwise, the kind of preaching were a matter of entire indifference.

Our object then is to determine the best methods of influencing men; or, in other words, to ascertain what are the conditions of power in the pulpit, in its human aspect. These conditions may be classified under three heads—the *matter*, the *manner*, and the *man*.

1. The Matter

If we are to influence the mind, we must have something to do it with. And to do this successfully, we must use *truth*—must speak according to *facts*. The mind assents to what it perceives to be true. Its constitution requires this. It is adapted to what is true, and is moved by it, as is the lock by the key. And it refuses to be moved by perceived untruth. If there is mistake in the statement, or fallacy in the reasoning, and this is seen, argument is useless. Speech has then no power.

But in preaching, *religious* truth is the instrument. The preacher is the appointed student and teacher of God's Word. And if he would have power, he must 'preach the word'. A peculiar energy attends that Word. It is the 'sword of the Spirit'; the 'fire', and the 'hammer that breaketh the rock in pieces'. It is 'quick, and powerful, and sharper than any two-edged sword.' It is 'perfect, converting the soul,' and 'making wise the simple.' Human philosophy, the wisdom of the world, has never converted a soul. It tried, and tried in vain, even to subdue the passions, and reform the life. But where the gospel goes, it demolishes the heathen temples, and sets up the reign of God. It proves itself to be 'the power of God unto salvation.'

Strong preachers have ever been Bible-preachers. The old Reformers drew their weapons from the heavenly armoury. The sermons of Bunyan, and Baxter, and Flavel, and men of their stamp, were full of God—instinct with living doctrines. Their very garb was after the Scripture pattern. Whitefield, as a custom, read the Bible with Matthew Henry's Commentary, day by day, on his knees, praying over every sentence, line, and word. Edwards and Davies were mighty in the Scriptures. Of Chalmers, it has been said, that his sermons 'held the Bible in solution.' Preachers who saturate their sermons with the Word of God never wear out. The manna which they bring is pure, and sweet, and freshly gathered. It never cloys. God's Word is deep, and he who studies it will ever have something new. He will never be dull, for the words of the Bible are strong, living words, and its images and descriptions are very flowers of elegance. Apt citations clench the passages of the preacher's discourse, and give sanction, dignity, positiveness, authority to it. And they shed light into his subject, like windows in houses, while to most of his hearers, certainly to the pious of them, these 'very words' of the Holy Spirit are delightfully edifying. They come like sweet-throated birds with a melody to the soul. 'I dearly love the sound of Scripture in a sermon,' said an old minister. Who does not? We recall some of the fathers in the ministry—men of one book—the scriptural element of whose sermons (faulty in some respects) made them very gardens of spices. The people loved to hear them preach, because their discourses had the smell of the myrrh and the cassia in them.

Few preachers would not be more weighty if more scriptural. A writer asks, 'Do ministers read the Bible much?' The question itself is startling. It is said of George Müller, author of *The Life of Trust*, whom all admit to be at least a man of God, and whose preaching has been greatly blessed, that 'he rises early, enters his closet, shuts the door, opens his Bible, offers a short prayer, especially to invoke the guidance of God's Spirit upon the reading and meditation of his holy Word, then reads and meditates verse by verse, chapter by chapter, till his soul becomes wholly impressed with God's presence and impregnated with God's teachings.' Let those who would have power in the pulpit, pursue a similar course.

But mere scripturalness does not make a strong sermon. Otherwise the recitation of inspired passages were sufficient. There must be *thought* as well. Men like to be made to think. They go to church to be instructed. The preacher, then, as a prime condition, must have something to say. It will not do to be always

> Dropping buckets into empty wells,
> And growing old in drawing nothing up.

A great want of most sermons is want of matter. In this age of mental activity and general intelligence, vigorous thinking and solid sense are absolutely necessary to permanent pulpit success. Intelligent people will tire of words, words, words, and demand *ideas,* and be apt to go where they can find them.

And again, as to matter in preaching, he who would have power must dwell much upon the two great, all-comprehensive doctrines of the Scriptures—man a *sinner,* and Christ a *Saviour.* Hence, the *law* will be used as an effective instrument; for 'by the law is the knowledge of sin.' A full conviction of sin, says John Owen, is 'a great and shaking surprisal unto a guilty soul.' This 'shaking surprisal' is the first thing to be gained. One must weep because of the 'curse' with which the Old Testament closes, or his eye will not be caught by 'the book of the generation of *Jesus Christ,*' with which the New Testament opens. He must be taken by the hand and led up to the top of 'stormy Ebal,' or he will never be ready to fly to the 'sun-lit height of Gerizim.'

The law must therefore be preached—it is indispensable to the authority and cogency of the pulpit—but not so much the law as the *gospel*—chiefly the *cross* of *Christ.* It was unto 'the *gospel* of God' that Paul was 'separated'. *Shiloh* is the great attraction, and to 'him shall the gathering of the people be'.

'And I, if I be lifted up, will draw all men unto me.' The heart will yield to the power of the cross, when it will yield to nothing else. We are told of an old emblem in the shape of a lock, constructed of rings, on each of which was a letter, and which would unlock only when those rings were so disposed as to spell the word *Jesus*. Apt emblem of the human heart. Was one *ever* known to open except to the name of *Jesus?* Chalmers was not the only preacher who had spent years in laboriously describing vice and virtue, and urging men to be better, and all to no effect, simply because there was no 'cross' in his preaching. And it is undoubtedly a chief defect in the sermons even of evangelical pulpits, that there is not enough of *Christ* in them. Pious people complain of this, especially in the sermons of those just from the 'schools,' and not without cause. The criticism of a certain theological professor upon the trial sermon of a student in the seminary, would apply to a multitude of the *moral essays* read from our pulpits: 'Young man, an educated *heathen* could write just as good a sermon as that!' It is a historical fact that the most successful ministers, in any age or country, have been those who determined, with Paul, to know nothing 'save Christ and him crucified.' Beyond question, Flavel was right: 'The excellency of a sermon lies in the plainest discoveries and liveliest applications of Jesus Christ.'

2. *The Manner*

From the *matter* of preaching, let us now turn to the *manner*. The word manner is here used both as to the *structure* and the *delivery* of a sermon.

1. Pulpit power is affected by the *composition* of a sermon. There is a right way and a wrong way of doing or saying anything. Everyone knows that the form of a communication affects its strength. A writing containing the same matter may

be either weak or strong, attractive or repulsive, eloquent or tame. And without being minute as to all the features of effective discourse, it will be found true that *plainness, simplicity,* and *directness,* are its prime qualities. The first thing is to be *understood*; to have the words and sentences intelligible. Paul had rather speak 'five words with the understanding,' *i.e.,* so as to be understood, 'than ten thousand words in an unknown tongue.' It is much easier to be unintelligible than intelligible. 'Ah, my brethren,' said Archbishop Usher, 'how much learning it takes to make things plain.'

Christ was the plainest preacher in the world. The apostles used 'words easy to be understood', and avoided things which 'minister questions rather than godly edifying'. So did the earnest men of God in any time. Ask Luther—whose words were 'half-battles'—how he preached and he will tell you it was not in a way to suit the 'learned men and magistrates,' of whom he had many as hearers, but for 'the poor, the women, and children, and servants,' of whom he had many more. See how the staunchest of the old Puritan divines of the seventeenth century preached, and it will be found that it was in the homely dialect of the common working people. One may read pages, and find scarcely a word of more than two syllables. Learn how the founders of Methodism preached; by Wesley's direction, they were to 'use the most common, little, easy words in the languages.'

A man who cannot make things plain is not qualified to fill a pulpit. First of all, let the preacher think out his subject so thoroughly that his ideas shall lie clear and distinct like crystals in his own mind; and then let him remember that 'a straight line is the shortest distance between two points,' and speak accordingly. What right has he to use an involved and tortuous manner when declaring the great things of God? When the late young preacher, Erskine Hawes, was dying, he said, 'I wish to live *to preach the gospel more simply.*' How many at death's door have felt as he felt?

We would not be understood to discourage the utmost care in the construction and preparation of sermons. Man is an organ, and skill is required to touch rightly the keys. *Method* is important. 'The preacher,' it is said, 'sought out and *set in order* acceptable words.' Thoughts, however good, and words, however plain, may be thrown together in such a desultory and irregular manner as to make no impression.

> Checked reason halts, her next step wants support;
> Striving to climb, she tumbles from her scheme.

The mind was not made to take in and hold a mob of ideas, a mass of unshapen materials. The thoughts of a discourse, therefore, must be 'set in order.' *Attractiveness,* too, is important. There is force in beauty and in every variety of wise and earnest speech. The good sense, and the taste, and the imagination of hearers are not to be ignored, but rather turned to advantage. Words wisely chosen are often images of things, awakening at once many ideas, and so coming with a wealth of beauty and meaning. Christ's preaching was attractive. His discourses are gemmed with beautiful metaphors and analogies, taken, however, not from the arts, but from nature, and familiar to all. Let style then be cultivated. What is complained of is the cultivation of elegance of imagery and felicities of diction, at the expense of simplicity and pungency. 'Prettiness is *not* in place in the pulpit.'

The eloquence needed for this age is that of Pericles, which 'left stings behind.' Most hearers know enough; they want to be made to *feel* and to *do.* The defensive outworks of Christianity are pretty well raised; we now need to advance on the enemy, and 'shell' him out from his entrenchments, by shooting fires into the souls of men. It were a blessing to some ministers who have so much 'dignity' to support, and who are so 'proper,' and so 'precise,' as to break nobody's heart with the hammer of truth, if Claus Harms[2] were to cry out in their ears, as to some of the 'fine writers' of his day, *'Speak negligently and incorrectly!'* A discourse had better be like a hetchel with the tow pulled out,[3] than like a damask cushion for the hearer to lean a sleepy head upon. Better like lightning, darting zig-zag, and piercing, and tearing, and splitting the object it strikes, than like a letter despatched without a direction (to use John Newton's comparison), addressed to nobody, owned by nobody, and if an hundred people were to read it, not one of them would think himself concerned in its contents.

Sermons are wanted now which are made and meant to *do execution* — sermons which grasp, and make bare, and wield some one mighty idea, holding it up, and turning it around, and repeating it, if need be, as does Demosthenes the one main point in his oration on the crown, until it becomes a palpable thing, and the audience *feel* its form and pressure — sermons having the 'agonistical,' the *wrestling* element in them, as Aristotle calls it — sermons put together on the principle that 'force in writing consists in the maximum of sense with the minimum of words', whose sentences are pounded together until they crack, and where figure, trope, allegory, metaphor, antithesis, interrogation, anecdote — *anything* that can awaken interest and deepen impression is resorted to — sermons supported and sinewed with the 'thus saith the Lord', and then charged with living truth, and aimed *directly at the conscience and the heart*, singling out each hearer, and saying, *'Thou art the man,'* and 'I have a message from *God unto thee,'* and then making pursuit after that man, in clear, rapid, concentrated utterances, and pressing upon him, and narrowing his way, and hemming him

[2] Claus Harms (1778–1855) German clergyman and theologian whose vigorous preaching style made him very popular in his day.

[3] A 'hetchel' is a comb-like tool used to separate fibres from the flax in the production of linen. 'Tow' flax is a very coarse, low-grade fibre, a remnant of the combing process.

in, and smiting him down with terrible volleys, until, quivering and breathless, he crouches 'between the law that condemns and the cross that saves'.

These are the sermons most needed to give power to the pulpit.

2. Upon the *delivery* of sermons, but little can here be said. God's wisdom is seen in giving prominence to *preaching*—to the *oral* communication of his Word. And he did not ordain preaching to do what the printing press could do as well. He designed that *men* should utter the truth, with the advantages of intonation, gesture, look. And they reflect upon God's wisdom who undervalue a good manner. It is easy to sneer at oratory, and inveigh against the study and practice of the art of elocution. But why not denounce art in *singing*, as well as in *speaking*? If all must be left to nature in one case, why not in the other? Nature does not despise art. It is the office of art to lead back to nature. The rules of oratory are all drawn from nature, if they are right rules; and he who practises upon them is only conforming to nature. It is time the vulgar prejudice against ministers learning how to be public speakers were done away with. In a very important sense *manner is matter*. And instead of less attention being given to this in ministerial training, there ought to be very much more. Neglecting this is like teaching cadets in a military school how to make powder and swords, but not teaching them how to *use* them. Many a minister fails, not from want of ammunition (for he has plenty of that), but because he cannot 'discharge' with effect the well-loaded weapon. His sword (to change the figure) is of the true metal, skilfully forged, and tempered and polished, but he does not know how to stand up and wield it. Let two ministers preach precisely the same sermon. In one case the hearers are cold, unmoved, inattentive. In the other they are attracted, convinced, melted. The difference was in the delivery. Who then will deny that, in some sense, manner is matter?

What power is there in the *voice,* when skilfully managed! It has been said of Whitefield that his 'Hark! hark!' could conjure up Gethsemane with its faltering moon, and again awake the cry of horror-stricken innocence; and an apostrophe to Peter on the Holy Mount would light up another Tabor, and drown it in glory from the opening heavens. All the authorities agree that a principal source of Whitefield's wonderful power was a voice of the richest compass, subject entirely to his control. Much may be done towards the acquisition of a distinct, strong, sonorous, flexible voice, where it is not natural; and too much attention cannot be given, in its training, to the modulation, or inflection, or varying of the voice, to avoid monotony, and make it the docile and faithful interpreter of the thoughts. It is certainly a sacred duty of every minister to bring to their highest perfection the organs of speech.

There is power, too, in a *smile,* or a *frown;* in the 'sweet, silent rhetoric of persuading *eyes,'* and in the glow of the *features,* or their solemn sadness. Doubtless, it was not with the same expression of countenance that he who spake as never man spake, cried, 'Woe unto you, scribes and Pharisees, hypocrites!' and 'If any man thirst, let him come unto me and drink.' There is power in *gesture,* to help the eye to anticipate each rapid utterance, and to deepen its effect. There is power in an *animated* manner. One's whole appearance in preaching may be either inspiring to an audience, or absolutely soporific; and we agree with another, that nothing can be more indecent than to hear 'a dead preacher speaking to dead sinners the living truth of a living God'. So is there power in an *affectionate* and *winning* manner — a fine example of which was the late Robert Murray M'Cheyne. And *whatever* pertaining to delivery that is excellent and of good report, should be earnestly coveted, as among the 'best gifts.'

3. The Man

We now come to those conditions of pulpit power which pertain to the *man* himself — to his inner or essential being. It is common to suppose that eloquence is a thing to be put on, that it is an outward affair. No mistake could be greater. In impressive public address, it is not so much the mouth that speaks as the soul; not so much the manner as the sentiment and the thought which creates the manner. The power consists in the action of the speaker's *soul* on the soul of the hearer. The elocutionist cannot make a preacher. The *man* must be made first. Behind what he can touch must be something to *beget* eloquence, or he might as well attempt to train an automaton. The foundation for successful public speaking, then, lies in the man himself. What is this foundation?

Goodness must lie at the bottom. The word is used in a broad sense to include piety, and moral excellence, and uprightness. The ancients had a maxim that no one could be eloquent but a good man. 'An orator', said Cato, the censor, to his son Marcus, 'is a good man skilled in speaking.' And we read in another of the ancients, 'Every man speaks as he lives.' 'A minister's life,' says an old divine, 'is the life of his ministry.' The explanation is obvious. Weight of character (depending on real goodness) gives weight to words; while supposed insincerity, and known inconsistency of conduct, neutralize all that one can say.

Knowledge also lies at the base of pulpit power. How can one teach unless himself taught? How can he accomplish his persuasion without acquaintance with language, and its relation to thought, and a delicate perception of the laws of association, by which what is said shall suggest 'that richer part of wisdom which must for ever remain unsaid?' A novice cannot even command respect. It is indispensable that a minister be well instructed in the *Scriptures,* and he should not be ignorant of the *sciences*. He should know *men,* too, as well as books. Many ministers are altogether too 'bookish.' They fail of influence from not knowing the material they have to operate upon. The heart of man must be interpreted, as well as the Word of God, by him who would have power over an audience. He must be thoroughly acquainted with human nature—must know the feelings of men of all classes and conditions, and all the springs of action, and avenues to the soul. He is the best preacher, says one whose own success ought to qualify him to speak, 'who has the best knowledge of human nature—not of the philosophy of mind in the abstract, though that is important—but of the wants, the susceptibilities, the struggles, the temptations, the reasonings, the shifts of individual minds in regard to religion.' So, also, should the preacher be able to scan the material world with a keen, discriminating eye. C. H. Spurgeon affords an example of the advantage of sensibility to the visible creation. Having occasion not long ago to prepare a sketch of his life, a note was addressed to him with this question: 'Where were you educated?' To which he answered, 'Nominally at divers schools in Newmarket; really by *summer rambles,* hard *private studies,* and *close observation.*'

Courage in a preacher is necessary to pulpit power. It was when the people saw 'the boldness of Peter and John' that they marvelled, and 'took knowledge of them that they had been with Jesus.' And Paul desired his brethren to pray that he might open his mouth 'boldly' in preaching the gospel. Our Master taught 'with authority.' Authority is inherent in truth. We expect one who knows he is in the right to speak with boldness; and Vinet, in his *Homiletics*, remarks, with truth, that the accent of authority is welcome to almost anyone. We are prepossessed in favour of men who, in this world of uncertainty and perplexity, express themselves on a grave subject with confidence and command. Some preachers weaken their messages by an indecisive mode of statement, giving the impression that they are either careless, or timid, or half-persuaded. They qualify and guard everything, as if somebody would take exception. Instead of this, they should come saying, 'We are the servants of the Most High! These are *his* words—not ours; and not one jot or tittle will we abate from them, nor give subjection to opposers, no, not for an hour!' Men dealt with thus fearlessly, acknowledge the preacher's power. His courage energizes and inlocks his thoughts, and gives to them decision, majesty, strength.

Experience is necessary to an impressive preacher. There are different ways of learning things. Some of our knowledge is intuitive, or ideal—a matter of pure reason. Some is speculative, gathered by deduction or inference. Some is the result of reading; some of instruction. But another kind, and quite different from all this, is that which we acquire by experience. And this knowledge is deepest and most actual. It is 'burnt in,' and becomes a part of our energies and powers. Now preachers want this kind of knowledge. It is needful that they be able to say, 'We have seen and felt; *therefore* we believe.' 'We speak that we do know, and testify that we have seen.' It is an old saying that the wounded is the wounding heart. One always speaks most strongly of what he has felt. Indeed, in successful discourse, one cannot go much beyond that. When the preacher is ready to cry out with Elihu of old, 'I am full of matter; the Spirit within me constraineth me; I will speak that I may be refreshed'—then look out for a torrent of irresistible utterance! Could Luther have been the giant he was in the conflict with hell, had he not felt beforehand the cogs of his terrible experience, striking him through and through, and well nigh tearing him asunder? He *knew* what he talked about. Those inward torments, compared with which the tortures of the stake were as nothing, were an essential part of his education. Hear what Bunyan says about the way he preached: 'I preached what I felt; what smartingly

I did feel; even that under which my poor soul did groan and tremble to astonishment. I went myself in chains to preach to them in chains; and carried that fire in my own conscience, that I persuaded them to be aware of.' And it was equally true of the blissful experiences which he describes. Could Baxter have written his *Saint's Rest* except for that long and weary sickness of his in a solitary chamber in Derbyshire? It was a transcript of his own heart, and hence it had, as he says, 'the greatest force on the hearts of others' of all his writings. Hence we see that a minister must draw from the depth of his own soul if he would have power in the pulpit. And this is why God lets so many candidates for the ministry struggle and suffer as they do. 'It is of difficulties that miracles are born,' says La Bruyère. And so God environs with inward and outward difficulties his young servants, that they may grow strong and know something for themselves! And this amazingly helps them to preach. Their discourses are apt to be woven and wrought out of a feeling heart, and to have definite points in them, and to come home to men's souls.

Industriousness lies at the base of pulpit power. We use it here as equivalent to *hard study*. Ordination does not bring omniscience. The pulpit has no magic to infuse wisdom. And previous culture is not a stock for a lifetime. One may have a transient popularity without study; but the cistern soon runs out, and the people get tired of drivelling and sediment. It is too late, now, to talk of God's helping those who do not help themselves. Though he made the beast of Balaam to speak, he will not countenance men in laziness. If he does not need our wisdom, he certainly does not our stupidity. It is an insult to God to go idly up and down all the week (or all but Saturday!), and then on Sunday bring an offering to the Lord 'which cost us nothing,' 'the blind, the lame, the sick,' 'a corrupt thing for sacrifice,' and ask God's blessing upon it. How can such preaching have power?[4] 'Give attention to *reading*'; '*study* to shew thyself approved,' says Paul. Without this, a Samson in native talent will soon lose his locks. A strong preacher *must* keep his mental powers in working order. He *must* be a man of rigid, unremitted diligence. He *must* plough, and cross plough, and subsoil his own mind, that it may yield nourishment to other minds.[5]

Sympathy is an element of strength. We want to see a *brother* in one who undertakes to do us good: hence if a man is persuaded that you really *love* him, you can do almost anything with him.

Enthusiasm is essential to power in the pulpit. Every eminent man is an enthusiast in his profession. He thinks there is no calling like it. And he who would not esteem it a self-degradation to exchange his pulpit for a throne, is not fit to fill a pulpit. Said the venerable William Carey, when the Rangoon government had placed his son in a dignified and important office, 'My son is shrivelled from a missionary into an ambassador.' The dignity and magnitude of the preacher's calling should so rise upon his vision as to shut out all else. He should live, and move, and have his being for one thing—to magnify his office, to fulfil his ministry. Thus enthusiastic, he cannot be tame. Handel caught the idea of one of his great choruses from the ring of a blacksmith's hammer and anvil. Talma, the tragedian, took a hint from the impassioned but restrained conversation of a group of men, which changed the entire style of theatric

[4] 'Live for your sermon; live in your sermon. Get some starling to cry Sermon! sermon! sermon! The best discourses are the efflux of a man's best thoughts and feelings during the week.'—*J. W. Alexander.*

[5] 'If the minister labours not to increase his stock, he is the worst thief in the parish. It is wicked for a man trusted with the improving of orphans' estates to let them lie dead by him; much more for a minister not to improve his gifts, which I may call the town-stock given for the good of the souls of both rich and poor.'—*William Gurnall.*

delivery. Chalmers riding on a stage-coach, and seeing the driver whip one of the horses to prevent his taking fright at an object in the distance, resolved the matter into a principle, and upon it developed his famous sermon on '*The expulsive power of a new affection*.' These men were enthusiasts, each in his profession, and everything subserved their ends. And so it will be found with any minister who is thoroughly absorbed in his profession. He is learning out of the study as well as in the study. When he goes abroad to breathe God's sweet air, and survey his beautiful world; when he mingles in society, and watches what is going on in the world, he is adding to his stock of ideas. Everything is feeding the sources of eloquent thought. Like the bee, he is gathering honey wherever he rambles, to bring back to his pulpit-hive. Each day of the week he is preparing to feed his flock, and not the least thing, in his reading or observation, that can add to the requisite material, is allowed to escape untreasured. Thus from a living enthusiasm he waxes strong.

Earnestness, an element closely allied to the latter is also requisite. The earnest man is intent on carrying his point. He has an *aim*, and his hearers *feel* it when he comes in contact with them. It was this that wrung from the lips of Agrippa, 'Almost thou persuadest me to be a Christian.' Eminent orators are always earnest speakers. When Dr Mason returned from Scotland, he was asked wherein lay Chalmers' strength. 'In his blood-earnestness,' he replied. A simple Scotch woman's description of M'Cheyne's preaching told the secret of his effective appeals: 'He preached as if he was dyin' a'most to have ye converted.' What an increase of pulpit power if all preachers spoke with a like earnest purpose! We need men more like Christ, whose soul was all sensibility; more like Paul, who 'travailed in birth again' for immortal souls; men after the stamp of good John Welsh—son-in-law of John Knox—whose weeping would sometimes awaken his wife, whose surprise he relieved by saying,

'O woman, I have the souls of three thousand to answer for, and I know not how it is with many of them!'; men who could say to their flocks with Rutherford, 'My witness is above, that your heaven would be two heavens to me, and the salvation of you all as two salvations to me;' and with Brainerd, 'I cared not where or how I lived, or what hardships I went through, so that I could but gain souls to Christ. While I was asleep, I dreamed of these things, and when I waked the first thing I thought of was this great work.' A new day will dawn upon the churches, when, in answer to their prayers, a race of ministers thus earnest shall come into possession of their pulpits.

Passion is essential to the greatest effectiveness. Deep feeling is contagious. It melts and wins its way. Sermons from burning hearts set others on fire. One of the best definitions of eloquence is, 'to have something to say and to *burn* to say it.' If the eloquence of art be not the eloquence of the heart, it is of little worth. Sermons fabricated in the furnace are very different from sermons constructed with the cold-chisel and file. Preaching should by no means be purely emotional; nor yet should it be purely intellectual. Paul will not be suspected of mental imbecility, nor of fanatical weakness; but mark what he said to the Ephesian elders: 'Remember that by the space of three years I ceased not to warn everyone of you, night and day, *with tears.*' Let cold, heartless, 'intellectual' preachers ponder this statement of Paul! Other things being equal, a man's force in this world is always just in the ratio of the force of his heart. A full-hearted man is generally a powerful man. As a rule, no man can be a great preacher without great feeling. His message, like the dart of Acestes,[6] must kindle as it is shot forth. Examine the past and the present, and the men of mark will be found to be men of the mighty heart. Let those, then, who would have

---

[6] Trojan ruler of Sicily. During the archery event of a competitive games, his arrow miraculously catches fire in mid-air (Virgil, *The Aeneid*, Book V).

power in the pulpit, aim at a high degree of subdued passion. Let them see that their altar-candle, besides being orthodox and straight, is made to *burn;*—that their production, besides having body, has also *soul;* and in delivering it, let them be sure that the heart palpitates on the paper.

Prayer is necessary to pulpit power. It is said of Pericles that he never ascended the rostrum without invoking the gods; much less should we without prayer. It was the deliberate opinion of an eminent minister that even aesthetically considered, one hour of prayer is a better preparation for sermon-writing than a whole day of study. One *cannot* make an edifying sermon while the heart is motionless. He *must* have the internal instruction of the Spirit, granted in answer to sincere supplication. 'We will give ourselves to *prayer,* and to the ministry of the word', said the apostles. Prayer, as one argues from this passage, is one-half of a man's ministry; and it gives to the other half all its power and success. It is incredible how much of light, vigour, strength, sprightliness, will come to the mind from a few moments' direct communion with God. Rightly spake Edward Payson of ministers: 'It is in the *closet* that the battle is lost or won.'

Faith is essential to powerful preaching. '*We believe,*' says Paul, '*therefore* we speak.' He who believes implicitly, will feel deeply and speak forcibly. Chrysostom, to help him in composing sermons, imagined the communion rails around the pulpit crowded with listening angels. Charles Simeon kept the picture of the flaming Henry Martyn hanging in his study, that it might seem to say to him, 'Be in earnest! don't trifle! don't trifle!' and the good Simeon would gently bow to the speaking picture, and say, 'Yes, I *will* be in earnest; I will *not* trifle: for souls are perishing, and Jesus is to be glorified.' But to the man of faith, there is present more than listening angels, or a sainted martyr, even the omniscient Master himself; and his voice is heard saying, 'Be thou faithful! Work while the day lasts! Entreat with all long-suffering and tears!' and under its influence, how can he loiter? how can he preach but with the tenderest importunity? Summerfield, on his death-bed, exclaimed, 'Oh, if I might be raised again, how could I preach! for *I have had a look into eternity!*' But faith affords such a look into eternity. Future things become present. The very surges of eternity seem beating against his study door. The Judge is actually coming! The worlds are burning! The heavens are departing! The throne is set! The books are open! The questions are being put—to *him,* and to his *flock!* and the angels are placing *these* on the right hand, *those* on the left! *There* is heaven with its rapturous songs, and myriads of shining ones; and *there* is hell, with its

> . . . groans that end not, and sighs
> That always sigh, and tears that ever weep,
> And ever fall, but not in mercy's sight:

and with all this before him, it is impossible to be unmoved. His spirit is stirred within him, and he exclaims—'No! these souls shall *not* commit suicide!' And, after first crying to God on his knees, he goes into his pulpit, and cries out to *them;* and there is nothing that is strong in argument, or sweet in entreaty, or thrilling in appeal, that he does not seize upon, and appropriate to his mighty theme. Thus does faith give him power.

Holiness is essential to pulpit power. This is placed last because most important. Our blessed Lord said to his apostles, 'Ye shall receive power *after that the Holy Ghost is come upon you;*' and he gave command that, when he should be taken up from them, they 'should not depart from Jerusalem, but *wait for the promise of the Father.*' They were not qualified to preach until the Divine Spirit, *in a special sense,* had come upon them. Neither is anyone. This alone can bring the preacher into such relations to God, and to men, and to his work, as will ensure success. The holy soul, only, is in close communication with the

Almighty, whence all his help must come. 'The secret of the Lord is with them that *fear* him, and he sheweth *them* his covenant.' He who lies in God's bosom draws from 'the hiding-place of his power,' both the wisdom to know, and the strength to wield, the Word of truth. God teaches him the deep things of the kingdom, and clothes him with superhuman energy. Some can readily be recalled who have walked among us in other days, as burning and shining lights, because of their peculiar sanctity. In one sense, they were not learned and eloquent; in another sense they were. Their fellowship was with the Father and with his Son Jesus Christ, and they were most acceptable and useful preachers. Their sermons were fetched up from the depths of their souls. They were fresh. Even the texts they quoted seemed new, from having been steeped in their own experience. And with what unction, and pathos, and subduing goodness they delivered their messages!

It is common to disparage the present as compared with the past; but still it is a question worthy of the most serious consideration, whether the holiness of the pulpit in other days can be found among ministers now. Is there a man living that would not name, as the *first* requisite to increased pulpit efficiency, 'a new baptism of the Holy Ghost?'

How many men, now weak and common-place ministers, would become mighty in word and doctrine, if only 'filled with the Holy Ghost!' The people would wonder at them, as if made anew. Much as they who preach need many things, they need nothing half so much as more communion with God, more sympathy with Christ. They are comparatively feeble as *preachers*, because feeble as *Christians*. Their lips are not touched with 'the coal from the altar;' *therefore,* the hearts of the people do not 'burn within' them.

Let it be remembered, then, especially by those coming to the ministry, that the very first principle in the philosophy of *doing* good is to *be* good; that if one would have power in the pulpit, he must stand in the light of God's countenance, as the angel in John's vision stood in the sun. Let them be particularly watchful against a *professional* piety. It is easy to *appear* religious, to speak the language, and do the duties, and exhibit the feelings of religion, when it is merely *ex officio,* shadowy, mechanical. Awful thought, but true! Constant attention to religious subjects, and religious offices, is liable to induce insensibility. Professional duty becomes one's business, and spirituality in its performance is lost. Because engaged in holy things, the minister is esteemed holy; and he persuades himself that he is holy, and so lives on in this way, *forgetting* that a holy office does not make one holy; *forgetting* that he may be spiritual in his pulpit, and not in his closet; *forgetting* that he may be the keeper of others' vineyards, without keeping his own; *forgetting* that it is easier to declaim against sins in *others* than to mortify them in *himself;* aye, forgetting that he may be the instrument of grace to others, and yet himself be *lost!*

Let ministers take heed to these things. Let the startling language of Dr Owen ring in their ears: 'He that would go down to the pit in peace, let him obtain a great repute for religion; let him preach and labour to make others better than he is himself, and in the mean time neglect to humble his heart, to walk with God in a manifest holiness and usefulness; and he will not fail of his end.' And these still more startling words from Swinnock: 'It is a doleful thing to fall into hell from under the pulpit; but, oh! how dreadful is it to drop thither out of it.' Let all who minister in holy things see to it that they are thoroughly *honest* men, without *hypocrisy.* Let them taste the Word before they distribute it, and be able to say with the devoted Thomas Shepard, 'I have never preached a sermon to others, that I have not first preached to my own soul.' In so doing, they shall magnify their office. 'Clothed with humility', 'nourished up in the words of faith and sound doctrine', and 'filled with all the fulness of God', it shall not be so much they that speak as Christ who dwelleth in them; and their words shall most surely be 'with the demonstration of the Spirit, and with power.'

* * * * *

NOTE ON PREACHING AND PRAYER

Owen Jones in his Some of the Great Preachers of Wales, *(1885), gives the following valuable comment on the relation of prayer to the work of the preacher.*

A book has been written by Professor Mahaffy upon *The Decay of Modern Preaching*. He accounts for this decay by dwelling altogether upon what is subsidiary and comparatively unimportant. The decay of preaching does not arise from any plurality of causes, but from one great cause, the want of the Spirit of God. Civilisation, learning, discipline, and training, whatever effect they may have upon the human race, cannot in any way either dispense with the influences of the Spirit, or make men less susceptible to them.

To attribute the decay of preaching to external circumstances, is to forget the real source of pulpit power. We all admit there is a certain diminution of visible power, but it is certainly due to the men that fill the pulpits of the present day, and the churches they serve. It may be because they are not so thoroughly devoted to the work as the men of days that are gone. It may be because they depend too much upon the learning of the day; and attend too much to scientific questions; and, on the other hand, give less time and attention to communion with God and prayer. The son of John Elias, writing to *Y Drysorfa*, a monthly serial, comparing the preachers of the present day with their fathers, observes:

Look at the seraphic Robert Roberts, Clynnog, rolling on the floor of the hay-loft, weeping and praying. Why is the poor man in such agony? He is starting on one of his preaching journeys, and is anxious lest the Spirit of God be not with him to convert the world and edify the saints. His study is not a poor one, when we remember the times; but the Bible, expositions, and books are not sufficient, in his estimation, without the Spirit of God. Go to the Association at Llanerch-y-medd, and see the effect of this agonising in the hay-loft. The hunchback stands on the pavement in front of the Bull Inn, like the angel of God, and in the flood of Divine influences, he lifts up his eyes and hands to heaven, saying, 'Enough, Lord; withhold thine hand; I can stand no more!' Observe Mr Williams, Lledrod, a scholar, and good linguist, and see him on his knees beside the black hedges; it is there he finds the materials of his sermons. Morgan Howells disappears from his family on Saturday night; on Sunday morning he wakes them up early, and calls for his horse; he is now ready to go and preach his Master, for he believes that He will go with him. The great William Roberts, of Amlwch, would be in a cloud of gloom and depression, struggling with God, before delivering those sermons that swept over the devil's forces like a mighty overwhelming wind. And Mr Rees, who will ever be remembered with endearment and reverence, whose ministry opened and searched the recesses of my heart many a time—what is he doing in the lonely cellars of the Liverpool chapels? moving about, restless, bending his knees, writhing, rising up, walking about, and bending on his knees again! He has received a message from God to sinners, and he prays that he may be in the hands of God to deliver it effectively.

OTHER BOOKLETS IN THIS SERIES FROM
THE BANNER OF TRUTH TRUST

Abortion: Open Your Mouth for the Dumb Peter Barnes
The Authentic Gospel Jeffrey E. Wilson
Behind a Frowning Providence John J. Murray
The Bleeding of the Evangelical Church David Wells
Burial or Cremation? Does It Matter? Donald Howard
A Call to Prayer J. C. Ryle
Can We Know God? Maurice Roberts
The Carnal Christian Ernest Reisinger
Christians Grieve Too Donald Howard
Coming to Faith in Christ John Benton
The Cross: the Pulpit of God's Love Iain H. Murray
The Cross: the Vindication of God D. M. Lloyd-Jones
A Defence of Calvinism C. H. Spurgeon
Evangelistic Calvinism John Benton
Finding Peace with God Maurice Roberts
The Five Points of Calvinism W. J. Seaton
The Free Offer of the Gospel John Murray
Healthy Christian Growth Sinclair B. Ferguson
Her Husband's Crown Sara Leone
Holiness Joel R. Beeke
The Incomparable Book W. J. McDowell
The Invitation System Iain H. Murray
Jesus Christ and Him Crucified D. M. Lloyd-Jones

The Kingdom of God W. Tullian Tchividjian
A Life of Principled Obedience A. N. Martin
Living the Christian Life A. N. Martin
The Moral Basis of Faith Tom Wells
The Practical Implications of Calvinism A. N. Martin
Preaching that Gets Through Stuart Olyott
Preaching: the Centrality of Scripture R. Albert Mohler
The Priority of Preaching John Cheeseman
The Psalter—The Only Hymnal? Iain H. Murray
Read Any Good Books? Sinclair B. Ferguson
Reading the Bible Geoffrey Thomas
Reading the Bible and Praying in Public Stuart Olyott
Rest in God Iain H. Murray
Simplicity in Preaching J. C. Ryle
Study Guide for 'The Mortification of Sin' Rob Edwards
Study Guide for 'The Promise of the Future' Cornelis Venema
The Unresolved Controversy Iain H. Murray
Victory: The Work of the Spirit Pieter Potgieter
What Is the Reformed Faith? J. R. de Witt
What's Wrong with Preaching Today? A. N. Martin
Whom Shall I Marry? Andrew Swanson
Worship J. C. Ryle

OTHER TITLES ESPECIALLY FOR PREACHERS

The Banner of Truth Trust originated in 1957 in London. The founders believed that much of the best literature of historic Christianity had been allowed to fall into oblivion and that, under God, its recovery could well lead not only to a strengthening of the church but to true revival.

Inter-denominational in vision, this publishing work is now international, and our lists include a number of contemporary authors along with classics from the past. The translation of these books into many languages is encouraged.

A monthly magazine, *The Banner of Truth*, is also published and further information about this, and all our other publications, can be found on our website or by contacting either of the offices below.

THE BANNER OF TRUTH TRUST

3 Murrayfield Road,
Edinburgh, EH12 6EL
UK

PO Box 621, Carlisle,
Pennsylvania 17013,
USA

www.banneroftruth.co.uk